SEVEN
MAXIMUM CO

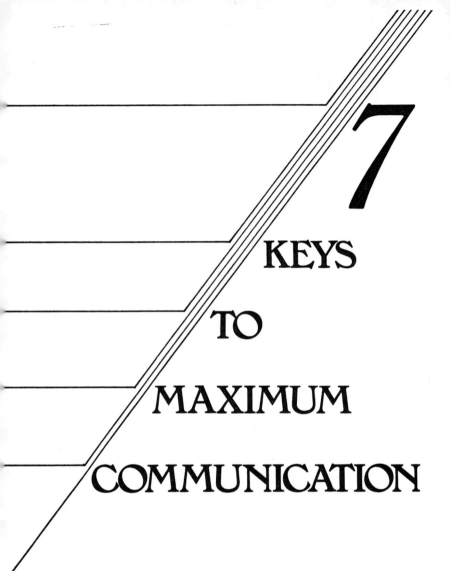

7 KEYS TO MAXIMUM COMMUNICATION

PAUL A. CEDAR

Tyndale House
Publishers, Inc.
Wheaton, Illinois

*Illustrations designed by
Mark John Cedar.*

*Library of Congress
Catalog Card Number
79-66820 ISBN
0-8423-5875-7
Copyright © 1980 by
Paul A. Cedar. All rights
reserved. First printing,
February 1980. Printed
in the United States of
America.*

To Jean, Dan, Mark, and Debbie—
who have been my most loving teachers
in the school of communication!

CONTENTS

THE SEVEN KEYS

CREATE THE MESSAGE

OVERCOME NOISE

MASTER LISTENING

MIRROR FEELINGS

UNDERSTAND AND PRACTICE LOVE

NOURISH AND LIVE DIALOG

ENABLED BY THE SOURCE

ONE:
AN INTRODUCTION

As I was brushing my teeth one day, our daughter Debbie, then about four years old, stood watching me with great interest. I decided to play a little game with her.

As the toothbrush moved back and forth within my mouth, I spoke to her, purposely distorting my speech so she wouldn't understand what I was saying. Then I took the toothbrush out of my mouth and asked her very distinctly, "What do you think of that, Debbie Jean?"

She looked puzzled and finally said, "I couldn't understand what you said."

I replied with tongue in cheek, "Listen a little more carefully this time."

Again I placed the toothbrush in my mouth, distorted my speech, spoke with great enthusiasm, removed the toothbrush, and asked, "Well, what do you think of that, Debbie Jean?"

This time she replied immediately, with some frustration, "Dad, I could hear you speaking, but I couldn't hear what you were saying!"

We often hear people speaking, but don't hear what they are saying. And even more frequently, we attempt to communicate clearly with others only to discover that they either do not understand what we are saying or else simply do not listen. How frustrating and painful!

That's what communication is all about—sharing common ideas, information, or experiences! The word "communication" is derived from the Latin word *communis*, which literally means "common." When we communicate, we are involved in sharing, harmony, accord, openness, union, and/or affinity.

Can you imagine a world in which everyone would be able to communicate without misunderstanding—just open, loving, clear, understandable communication? What a wonderful way in which to live—sharing in love and understanding with others. In truth, that would be Heaven!

Unfortunately, the antonyms of communication are experienced more frequently by most of us. Alienation, disunion, division, separation, disharmony, discord, and disagreement are the enemies of effective communication—and they prevent us from enjoying life at its best.

Communication is breaking down all around us. Family and marriage counselors state that communication problems are a major contributing factor to the escalating divorce rate and the subsequent number of broken homes. The same statement is made concerning other breakdowns in human relationships.

More is being communicated about communication in our society than any time in history, and yet communication difficulties appear to be increasing in epidemic proportions. Husbands and wives, parents and children, teachers and students, employers and employees, business and labor, government and taxpayers—all suffer from the painful disease of communicational discord.

What can be done to help us communicate more effectively? That is the $100,000 question! Interestingly, most of us believe that the problem is with other people. We hope that "they" will soon get things straightened out so that clear communication can flow between us. We wait for our parents, wives, superiors, and other persons in our lives to "shape up!"

However, if clear communication is to take place in your life, the solution must begin with *you!* We have passed the buck long enough. In fact, "passing the buck" is one of the greatest problems we face in solving our personal problems. Over the years, most peple who have come to me for marriage counseling have not come for personal help, but in order for me to correct their husband or wife's behavior—not their own. The same thing is true regarding our personal communication problems. We tend to blame others for our communication breakdowns rather than assuming personal responsibility for our own communication shortcomings.

It is time for you and me to do all that *we* can to become more effective communicators—so that we can enjoy the fulfilling life of maximum communication and share it with others! Only then can we become a vital key to the solution instead of a continuing contributor to the communications dilemma.

That's what this book is all about. It has been written so that you and I can become more effective communicators. Notice my emphasis on the word "become." Be assured that I have not attained the position of the "ultimate communicator." I am still in process, and I invite you to join me in the exciting adventure of striving to enjoy maximum communication.

There is no easy or quick solution to the communications crisis in most of our lives. In short, communication can be no more effective than are the persons involved in the communication process. We are talking about a people problem. That's why we need to begin with you—and me!

This book shares seven basic communications principles which can change your life. Reading the book will allow you to recognize and understand these principles, but that is only the first step.

Each chapter closes with some practical exercises for you to use along with your family and friends. These exercises will help you to assimilate the principles of maximum communication into your lifestyle. To *know* the truth is not enough; you must *practice* the truth until it becomes integrated into your daily walk.

You can be an effective communicator! The key word is "commune." The seven principles you will be mastering stem from that word. This book serves as a door through which you can enter this exciting life of communion, love, sharing, and openness—*maximum communication!*

I invite you to join me in exploring the seven keys of communication. Let us begin!

TWO:
CREATING THE MESSAGE

KEY #1: *CREATE THE MESSAGE. We must understand the basic components of communication in order to create an effective message.*

How would you define communication? Without realizing it, most of us would probably come up with some variation of what communication theorists refer to as the "conveyor belt" definition.

For most of us, communication is the process of transmitting information to another person. We have something which we would like another person to know or a command to convey to someone. And for us, that is communication!

Prime examples of this would be the parent who tells the teenager to carry out the garbage, or the husband who tells the wife what he would like for supper, or the employer who instructs his secretary how he would like a letter prepared. In each of these situations, information is transmitted from one person to another, and this message is given with definite expectations.

How simple the communication process would be if these were the only dynamics involved in communication. However, they certainly are not!

What if the teenager decides he does not want to

carry out the garbage and talks back to his parent? Or what if the wife is fed up with always preparing what her husband desires for dinner and decides to do her own thing? Or what if the secretary is busy and is "tuned out" to what her boss has to say? The answer to all of these questions is simple—there is a communication breakdown.

In the real world in which we live, there are many more experiences of communication breakdown than there are of effective communication. Communication is much more complex than merely transmitting information. You see, communication involves persons—not objects.

Effective communication requires not merely the transmission of information, but the sharing of a message; not only the sharing of a message, but the sharing of the meaning of the message; not only the sharing of the meaning of the message, but the sharing of life itself—which is communion.

But before we can begin to think about communication on such a deep and meaningful level, we must first understand its basic components and subsequently learn how to create a meaningful message.

FIGURE ONE:

BEGINNING WITH THE SOURCE

Communication always begins with a *source*. In short, communication can never be any more effective than the source. If the source is bad, the communication is bad. But if the source is good, the communication process has the potential of being good (depending upon other communication factors which we will be exploring together).

For example, if you make a recording which is very difficult to understand because of much background noise or because the volume is too low, it is impossible to improve its quality by duplicating that message to another tape. In fact, the recording will actually lose some of its quality and will be more difficult to understand than the original.

That is a basic premise of the communication process. Each time a basic message is communicated from one person to another, some of the purity of the original message will probably be lost. That is why written history is so much more reliable than oral history.

A perfect example of this premise is to be demonstrated in the little "gossip" game played by most of us as children. The person beginning the game would whisper a simple message into the ear of the person sitting next to him. In turn, that person would whisper the message which he heard into the next person's ear. This process would continue down to the end of the line. The final person would then communicate aloud the message which she had received. Usually the message communicated at the end of the line was far different than the original message.

A major factor was the clarity of the original message. If it was clear, precise, and easy to understand, it had a good chance of reaching around the circle and being communicated correctly.

In short, if one is to be an effective communicator one must learn to originate clear and definitive messages. If our message is unclear or ambiguous, the communication process has no chance of succeeding. If the source is bad, the communication is bad! (Later in this book we will deal with how we can communicate more clearly and effectively.)

FIGURE TWO:

THEN COMES THE TRANSMITTER

As the *source* is the originating communicator, the *transmitter* is the means by which the source sends his or her message. The transmitter for most of our interpersonal communication is our vocal apparatus. In other words, most of us communicate more frequently by speech than by any other means.

Within our society, there is a great deal of emphasis on being able to effectively communicate verbally. As a boy and as a young man, I stuttered very badly. When I was in high school I sometimes stayed home from school on days on which I knew I had to recite. As long as I live, I will never forget the pain and the embarrassment of knowing what I wanted to say but being unable to utter the words. I learned firsthand what it meant to be handicapped by not being able to transmit in an effective manner verbally.

However, there are other means of transmitting messages. Most obvious is that of writing. We live in a literate society which equips us to both read and write. We also can transmit messages by sight and touch and other nonverbal means which we will explore in more detail a little later in this chapter.

In short, the message must be transmitted clearly—but it must also be transmitted appropriately. For example, it is not appropriate to transmit a message to a friend who is deaf by calling her on the telephone. Nor is it appropriate to talk in conversational tones to a friend who has normal hearing, but is a block away from the communicator.

Transmitting to those who are deaf may require writing or employing sign language or simply enunciating clearly so that your lips may be read. Communicating with a friend who is blind may require the transmission of clear sound or the use of braille. And transmitting to those who are blind and deaf may require the utilization of a remarkable system of communication based upon the sense of touch.

Effective transmission must be clear and appropriate.

FIGURE THREE:

THE CHANNEL IS THE KEY COMMUNICATIONS LINK

The five senses—sound, sight, touch, smell, and taste—are the basic communication *channels*. They link the source and the destination.

The selection of the appropriate transmitter obviously determines the actual channel used in a given communication experience. For example, if the selected transmitter is the vocal apparatus, then the obvious channel is sound.

However, communication often utilizes more than one channel at a given time. For example, I will never forget a communication experience which I observed one day when debarking from an airplane at a major West Coast airport during the Vietnam War. A mother was waiting at the end of the walkway for her son, who was returning from Vietnam. She had her camera poised and ready.

However, when she saw her son she lost her poise. She dropped her camera, squealed with delight, ran down the walkway, and embraced her son with tears of joy. She was using all of the senses as channels of communication—sound, sight, touch, and probably even some smell and taste!

Just as the term implies, channels are merely the vehicle by which we communicate our message. The more channels we can use simultaneously, the more effective and understandable our message will be communicated.

For example, I can convey the message "I love you" by merely expressing it verbally. However, how much more meaningful that message is when it is given via the channel of touch through a physical embrace, the channel of sight through direct and loving eye contact, the sense of sound through the use of proper voice level and inflection, the sense of smell through the personal hygiene of being properly bathed and groomed, and even the channel of taste through the vehicle of a tender kiss. What a difference the combination of all those channels can make in our communication of the simple statement, "I love you!" The message comes alive.

FIGURE FOUR:

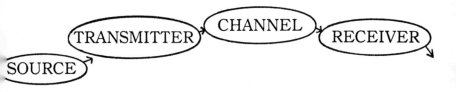

THE RECEIVER IS CRUCIAL

Not only must the transmitter and the channel be appropriate, but so must the receiver. If the transmitter is to be the vocal apparatus and the channel the sound waves, then the receiver must be the ear and the entire mechanism of hearing.

Our bodies have been given a number of receivers in addition to the ear, such as the eyes, the nose, the tongue, and our skin which receives the sense of touch.

It is crucial not only for the receiver to be appropriate, but also to be available and "tuned in." We do not hear a message simply because we have ears, nor do we receive messages merely because we are equipped to see, to feel, to smell, or to taste.

Availability is absolutely essential if the receiver is to function properly in the process of effective communication.

FIGURE FIVE:

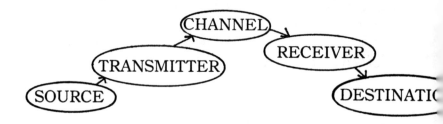

THE IMPORTANCE OF THE DESTINATION

If communication can be no more effective than its source, then it is equally true that it can be no more effective than its *destination.* In both cases, we are not speaking about objects, but about persons.

The source can communicate forever with clarity, appropriateness, and multi-faceted channels, but if the destination decided not to receive the message and not to respond to it, communication would never take place.

For example, imagine that in a rural area at 2:00 A.M. a disc jockey is sitting alone in a studio, talking and playing records. The electronic equipment is working properly and the transmitter is conveying the message over the airwaves at a given number of watts. But it is conceivable that although the source is good, the transmitter clear and appropriate, the sound waves working beautifully, there are no receivers turned on or tuned in—and therefore no communication is actually taking place.

This problem is faced by many teenagers who have found that though they try to speak and express themselves, their parents are simply too busy or too preoccupied to listen to them. And by many wives who feel that communication with their husband is impossible because of the morning newspaper or an evening television program. This kind of experience usually results in communicators feeling rejected or at best neglected. They often give up their attempts to communicate, and great barriers are raised which may lead to rebellious children and broken marriages.

Within our personal lives, this experience often takes place. We seem to speak, but no one listens; we write letters, but receive no response; we reach out to love and share, but no one seems to care.

Without a doubt, this is the most crucial and often painful realization in understanding the communication process. We can learn to be effective communicators, but unless the person who is the destination determines by his or her own will to receive the message and then respond, effective and meaningful communication cannot take place. Effective communication requires not only a good source and transmission, but also a good receiver and a responsive destination!

FIGURE SIX:

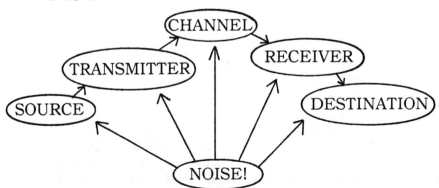

DON'T FORGET NOISE

The five basic components of the communication process, then, are: the *source*, the *transmitter*, the *channel*, the *receiver*, and the *destination*. But there are at least three other primary components which we must also consider.

For example, there is the matter of *noise*. Noise is anything which interferes with the communication process. You can have an ideal source, appropriate transmitter, correct channel, available receiver, and a sensitive and responsive destination and still not have effective communication, because some external or internal noise impairs or destroys the communication process.

Because noise is one of the greatest enemies of the meaningful communication process, we must constantly be alert to its cunning devices. Because it is so insidious, our next chapter will deal in depth with how to recognize and overcome both internal and external noise—that which comes from within us and that which attacks from outside of us.

Noise can interfere with communication at any one or at any combination of the five basic communication ingredients. If communication is to be effective, we must recognize and overcome any noise which would destroy or interrupt meaningful communication.

COMMUNICATION MUST HAVE A MESSAGE

Another vital component in the communication process is the actual *message*. If there is no message, there can be no communication.

Messages are basically communicated in two ways—*verbally* and *nonverbally*.

In short, the verbal message is what I say or write. This message can be spelled with appropriate letters or symbols or can be pronounced and enunciated in clear, understandable language. A

simple, clear example of a verbal message would
be, "I love you!"

But messages can also be communicated nonverbally. Nonverbal messages are essentially what I
do. There is an ancient proverb which summarizes
nonverbal communication well: "The character of
even a child can be known by his acts—whether
what he does is pure and right" (Proverbs 20:11,
TLB).

I can communicate genuine love to you not
merely by verbalizing that love, but by expressing
it physically with an embrace or kiss or by responding to your needs or by being faithful and
trustworthy. In fact, only with some kind of appropriate physical expression does the verbal message "I love you" become credible and practically
understandable.

That is a basic premise of authentic communication. Verbal messages are ultimately credible
when they are actively supported by appropriate
nonverbal messages. For example, love is not
merely a matter of talk, but of deed!

THE MEANING OF THE MESSAGE
Communication is the process of creating *meaning*.
Messages are transmitted verbally and/or nonverbally externally. However, meanings are not transmitted. Meanings are *translated internally*.

In other words, the same words and the same
verbal message can mean different things to different people. The translation of those messages
takes place inside of us. Out of this process comes
the meaning of a message.

For example, several years ago some friends of
ours adopted a precious little girl from Cambodia.
When we had the delight of meeting her, I instinc-
tively reached out to her with love and concern,
patting her on the head while uttering words of
welcome and affirmation.

Much to my surprise, she responded negatively

and with fear to my patting her on her head. Her new parents quickly shared the reason for her negative response. Within our culture, patting on the head denotes love and affirmation. However, in the Cambodian culture patting a child on the head is used to communicate disapproval or shame. I was attempting to communicate love and approval, but as the little girl translated the message internally her understanding of the meaning was one of shame and disapproval.

This communication factor becomes one of the greatest challenges faced in attempting to communicate effectively. We tend to assume that messages which are clear to us will be received and translated internally into meanings which are consistent with our intended purpose. Unfortunately they often are not!

This is the major reason why response and feedback are so important in communication. In another chapter we will deal much more specifically and practically with the important skill of feedback.

THE CHALLENGE OF EFFECTIVE COMMUNICATION

By exploring the eight basic components of communication, we have exposed some of the complexities and challenges facing us in interpersonal communication. There is little wonder that we have so many breakdowns in our daily communication and that we are so often misunderstood as we attempt to relate to others.

Effective communication is an art to be mastered. All of us possess the necessary tools. And although it is helpful to recognize the difficulties in communicating effectively, we should not become fatalistic or discouraged. To the contrary, we should commit ourselves to overcoming the obstacles and meeting the challenge.

This book will equip you to do just that! *You can become an effective communicator!*

SUGGESTED EXERCISES TO HELP YOU CREATE THE MESSAGE:

1. Memorize the basic components of the communication process.

2. Practice being the source in a conversation, with another person serving as the destination. Do your best to communicate your intended message just as clearly as possible. When you have completed sending your message, have the other person feed back the message to you as they received it. Discuss together any differences that may have occurred between the message which you sent and the one the other person received. Then attempt to determine the causes for the breakdown in communication.

3. Reverse roles with one another. Do your best to be the most effective receiver/destination which you can possibly be. As you practice the various roles, work on becoming just as effective a communicator as possible.

4. Attempt to assimilate the principles you learned in the exercises into your day-by-day lifestyle. At first, it will require your close attention since you will not only be focusing upon communicating your messages more clearly, but will also be breaking bad habits which have been formed over a long period of time. The more you practice and apply the principles which you have learned, the more effective your communication will become!

THREE:
OVERCOMING NOISE

KEY #2: *OVERCOME NOISE. We must overcome the noise that interferes with or blocks clear communication.*

Noise is anything that interferes with or blocks the accurate transmission and appropriate reception of a message. Noise is often in the form of sounds or sights or other externals, but it can also be internal feelings and attitudes. In fact, noise that affects communication can be placed in two major categories—external and internal noise.

EXAMPLES OF EXTERNAL NOISE

Sounds: In our everyday lives, we usually use the term noise to describe unappreciated or disturbing sounds. What is beautiful music to one person can be offensive noise to another. For example, I recently attended a concert at the famed Hollywood Bowl which had a mixture of contemporary rock and semi-classical music. Some older music lovers stood and literally shouted their disapproval at the rock musicians while others got up and marched out in protest. But many of the younger people were shouting and clapping in appreciation of the rock music. To them, rock was not noise—it was music at its best!

On the other hand, some desirable sounds become noise when they become too loud or when they are presented at an inappropriate time. For example, you may greatly enjoy Handel's famed "Hallelujah Chorus" in a concert hall, but it may become noise when it is blaring from a neighbor's stereo while you are trying to sleep.

In short, sounds become noise when they interrupt the communication process between two or more persons. They may be good, desirable sounds, but they become noise when they are inappropriate, unappreciated, or too loud for a given occasion.

Sights: Noise is not limited just to sounds. Sights can be a major source of noise when they interrupt the communication experience.

For example, several years ago I was invited to speak at a conference in a beautiful area of central Pennsylvania. The evening meetings were held in an outdoor pavilion. As I was beginning to speak on the first evening of the conference, a large flock of bats flew down from the rafters just above my head and swooped through the pavilion. Believe me, that was noise—without a word being spoken! Each succeeding evening, at approximately the same time, the bats would repeat their performance right on schedule, and that sight always interrupted what I was saying. That was noise!

I remember a second occasion when another sight dramatically interrupted the communication process. It took place during my senior year in college while I was taking a required history course taught by an outstanding professor from the old school. He believed in lecturing as the only method of education, and he lectured with great skill and gusto. He was past retirement age, but because of his excellence he was persuaded to continue teaching a few of his classes. He had become hard of hearing, and when lecturing he

would turn off his hearing aid so that nothing
would interrupt him.

One day a large dog entered the classroom.
Everyone seemed to notice it except the professor,
who simply kept on with his lecture. The dog was
extremely friendly, roving from one student to another.

The dog was noise in the classroom. Few students
were paying attention to our eloquent professor.

Any sight can become noise when it distracts or
interrupts the communication process. You and I
can become the noise of sight if we move inappro-
priately during conversation or behave in such a
way as to draw undue attention to ourselves while
another person is attempting to speak or share.

Language: Another potential source of noise is
found in language. If you speak English and if I
speak English, language is a proper and appropriate channel for meaningful communication. However, if you speak English and I understand only
German, language is no longer a channel—it has
become noise! Even dialects within the same language can become barriers to effective communication.

The language of communication must be mutually understood in order for it to become a channel
rather than noise.

Vocabulary: The same principle is also true in
relationship to vocabulary. For example, have you
ever heard a minister using a great deal of theolog-
ical vocabulary in his sermon so that his listeners
could not understand what he was talking about?
Or have you ever had a brilliant doctor attempt to
explain an illness to you, but he used technical
vocabulary of physiology which you could not understand? The problem was solved only when you
asked him to speak to you in "plain English!"

We live in a day of specialization, and most of us
use specialized forms of vocabulary which are not

readily understood by the general public. Therefore, our specialized vocabulary can be a barrier that blocks clear communication.

In other words, the vocabulary which we use in communicating to others must be appropriate, non-offensive, and mutually understood.

Symbols: Obviously the same principle must be followed in our use of symbols—both written and unwritten. Over the years, I have had a number of secretaries who were proficient in their use of shorthand. However, I have never learned to read or write shorthand. If someone were to write me a note and were to use the shorthand symbols, it would become noise since I simply could not understand it.

The same thing can be true of other symbols, such as religious or astrological symbols. They may be very meaningful to the user, but may be neither understood nor appreciated by others. They can become noise.

We need to use symbols which are mutually understood by the persons with whom we are communicating, so that the symbols may be channels for effective communication rather than the source of undesirable noise.

Body Position: Another source of noise can be our body position or body language. For example, have you ever attempted to visit with another person who is sitting with his head down and his eyes closed? To be sure, he may be concentrating on what you are saying, but such posture is usually a sign of disinterest and therefore becomes very loud noise.

Or have you ever attempted to communicate with someone who never looks at you, but is constantly looking away at other things and in other directions? Eye contact is extremely important in effective communication.

Of course, there are many other body positions which can become noise such as: a closed, defensive stance; a nonchalant, "I don't care" type of appearance; or a fidgeting, impatient type of posture.

Other External Noise: These are but a representation of the various possibilities of external noise. The list could go on and on.

For example, the way in which we dress can be noise—we can either overdress or underdress for an occasion. A tuxedo may be appropriate for a wedding, but would become noise at an office picnic.

My wife, Jeannie, and I were recently invited to a Halloween party which we understood was to be a costume party. When we arrived, we discovered that we were the only ones who were dressed in costumes. Needless to say, that was noise!

EXAMPLES OF INTERNAL NOISE

Although external noise is a constant enemy of effective communication, there is an even more dangerous enemy—internal noise. External noise can often be easily identified, dealt with directly, and overcome with minimal effort. However, internal noise is much more difficult to overcome because it takes place *within* persons. Internal noise can only be eliminated when we as persons acknowledge the presence of such noise and deal with it appropriately by an act of our will.

An Air of Superiority: An example of this insidious form of internal noise is to be found in persons who display an attitude of superiority. Most of us can envision examples from our own life experiences of persons who have related to us with such an attitude. One of my college classmates was constantly aloof in the way he communicated with and acted toward the other students. He literally kept his nose in the air as he walked through the campus. One day he walked right into a wheelbarrow a workman had placed on the sidewalk. Needless to say, he suffered a few bumps and bruises and a great deal of embarrassment. However, the greatest tragedy was that he continued to be a very lonely and alienated person. Effective communication between two people must always take place on eye level, even when one is better educated or a better athlete or of higher social status.

Some of the most humble, effective communicators I know have excelled in a given area of life, yet continue to communicate humbly to others. Success should not give us an air of superiority. It should make us grateful to God who gave us those innate abilities. Our successes should be shared openly and humbly with others to enrich their lives.

Every human being has unique gifts, abilities, and successes which should not become sources of noise, but rather should become channels to help and encourage people.

Meaningful communication cannot take place when one of the communicators displays the noise of an air of superiority.

Self-Centeredness: The same thing is true of a person who is self-centered. I have met people who can only talk and think about themselves and/or their families. Their basic vocabulary centers in the pronouns "I," "we," "me," and "mine." Most of us can think of people within the sphere of our lives who fall into this category. However, lest we merely see this trait in others, let us do a very thorough examination of ourselves and of our own vocabulary. How often we are more anxious to talk about ourselves or our families than we are to listen to others and their concerns! In such situations, we display self-centeredness rather than a spirit of love and caring.

Without a doubt, self-centeredness is a major curse of sin. Our society is permeated with persons who can never communicate "with" people, but can only talk "at" people.

These persons tend also to boast a great deal

(which reveals deep feelings of insecurity). They must compliment themselves since they receive so little from others. Their basic motivation is what they can "get" out of another person. They lust and desire and yet never seem to have that which ultimately satisfies—including a meaningful relationship with other persons.

Authentic communion or the sharing of life in deep and meaningful communication cannot take place when the noise of self-centeredness is present.

Dogmatism: Another enemy of communication is dogmatism. The roots of this evil form of noise also comes from insecurity. A classic picture of this deplorable trait is seen in a graphic definition of it recently shared with me by a friend: "Dogmatism in effect says, 'I will listen to no one else, because I know that I know best. My ideas are totally accurate.'" The dogmatic person must always be right and must always be "one-up" on other persons. He is the highest authority on a given subject; he can never be in error—he is infallible!

In short, he has become his own god. He cannot enjoy the risk of growing or learning and cannot risk being wrong or failing. He too speaks "at" people. His communication is one-way. Another person's input is only to be refuted or "put down" or "topped" by his own. Dogmatic people are lonely, empty, alienated people who can never enjoy sharing life with other persons.

Dogmatism stifles the light of communion and sharing; it offers only darkness and gloom.

Insensitivity: Becoming a sensitive, loving person is one of the most important characteristics of life and of effective communication. We will deal with the "how to" of becoming more sensitive and loving in a later chapter.

However, at this juncture it is important to recognize the noise of insensitivity. It is human nature to say or do your own thing without concern about responding to the feeling, moods, or needs of other persons. "I've done it my way!" will be the theme song of Hell.

As you have probably discovered, sensitivity is a characteristic which comes much more easily for some than others. Often we define it in terms of human temperaments or environmental background. However, I have discovered that sensitivity can be learned by even the most obnoxious and insensitive person. The key is in becoming as conscious and concerned about others as we are about ourselves. Very simply, when someone steps on my toe I recognize the pain immediately. I can and need to develop that same sensitivity to the pain and concerns of others. But such a degree of sensitivity requires a high level of effective communication.

Effective communication can take place only when we allow other persons to share their needs, moods, and concerns—and when they allow us to do the same. In turn, we need to respond to revealed selves with appropriate love and sensitivity.

Manipulation: Another major source of internal noise is the conduct we call manipulation. It is the kissing cousin of the aforementioned categories of internal noise.

Manipulation is using persons as objects in order to attain our desired goals. It can become a part of our lifestyle without our recognizing it clearly. For example, when I was in graduate school a fellow-student came to me and accused me of attempting to manipulate him. My initial response was one of hurt and disbelief. However, as I opened my heart and life to him and listened carefully, I discovered that indeed I had been trying to manipulate him. My motive had been right—I wanted what was best for him. But I was attempting to force that good upon him without his permission.

Manipulation is a form of rape. We force ourselves upon persons and then proceed to attempt
to squeeze them into our mold. Incredibly, we
often do this under the guise of love! Actually,
manipulation is human lust in one of its lowest and
most obnoxious forms.

Where there is manipulation, there cannot be a
mutual, loving, sharing of life, and therefore there
can be no meaningful communication.

Compulsive Speech: Have you ever tried to communicate with a person who speaks compulsively?
What an impossible task! Compulsive speakers are
self-centered, empty people. They are not concerned about sharing with other persons. They can
speak only "at" others.

I have met compulsive speakers who have mastered the art of not taking a breath for an hour. I
know because I spent an hour waiting for them to
take a breath, so I could respond to what they
were saying.

Compulsive speaking cannot be present in mutual sharing or in effective communication, except in
unusual situations where deep feelings need to be
ventilated and/or deep concerns need to be expressed.

A Judgmental Attitude: Some persons believe that
they have been appointed to be the critics of others. I have met people who actually believe that
God has given them the gift of criticism. I acknowledge the fact that they have become master
critics, but I can assure you that the gift did not
come from God! It is a result of their own sin and
selfishness. Most of these persons never seem to
criticize themselves—only others. Jesus spoke
very clearly about this problem when he warned
us against seeing "a speck in the eye of your
brother when you have a board in your own"
(Matt. 7:3, TLB). A judgmental attitude clearly
blocks open and loving communication.

Persons cannot openly share or communicate

with another when they fear that every word will be judged—and usually condemned. Self-appointed judges can never enjoy the adventure of communing with another person or of growing from such an experience. And, tragically, in the end judges are invariably judged by their own judgment.

Where there is a critical and judgmental attitude, there is noise in a most blatant and distasteful form.

Other Internal Noise: Again, the list of examples could continue for many more pages. In my opinion, internal noise is sin—and sin always leads to death! That is why internal noise never brings life to a relationship. It always brings darkness and alienation and emptiness and loneliness and frustration—and, ultimately, death!

Now the question becomes, How can I overcome this noise? How can I cope with external noise and also defeat the internal noises which would prevent me from enjoying life at its best—a life of love and growth and openness and transparency and interpersonal communion?

That, my friend, is what the remainder of this book is all about. The remaining five communication keys present the "how to" of maximum communication. The first two keys have revealed the need and the challenges for effective communication. Now let us proceed to some practical and workable solutions!

SUGGESTED EXERCISES TO HELP YOU OVERCOME NOISE:

1. Divide a sheet of blank paper into two columns. Head the left-hand column "EXTERNAL NOISE," and then list the specific forms of external noise which are the greatest challenge to your personal communication.

2. On that same sheet of paper, head the right-hand column "SUGGESTED SOLUTIONS."

Then attempt to write down very specific and practical solutions of how you can overcome each specific source of noise which you listed in the first column.

3.   Take a second sheet of paper and proceed with the same two-step process which you followed with the first. However, this time deal with "INTERNAL NOISE." Once again, be just as specific and practical as you can. Remember, in both exercises you are focusing upon the specific noises in your own life, especially those for which you are directly responsible.

4.   Share the above exercises with some of the people who are especially close to you and with whom you communicate on a regular basis, such as your spouse, your children, your parents, or your employer. For one week keep a written account of when you become responsible for "noise" as you communicate with these persons or others. Then discuss your discoveries with the key persons involved. Mutually attempt to determine how you can overcome this noise problem. Repeat this exercise until it becomes an integral part of your lifestyle.

FOUR:
MASTERING LISTENING

KEY #3: *MASTER LISTENING. We must master the art of empathetic and comprehending listening!*

You have probably discovered that there is a great deal of difference between hearing and listening. Hearing denotes simply the physiological ability to receive verbal messages from another source. However, in the vocabulary of the vernacular, the message may simply "go in one ear and out the other." In other words, you may hear a message but not take time to adequately understand it and respond to it.

In our society, for example, we are used to having background music. We hear it, but we are not concentrating upon it. We are not actually listening to it. Many young people have learned to do their studies while they have a radio or stereo blaring in the background. They are aware of the music, but they are not concentrating or listening to it with their conscious attention.

Listening is an art that has to be learned and mastered. Our lives would be greatly enriched if we mastered the art of empathetic and comprehending listening.

What prevents us from being good listeners?

There are at least five major categories of potential barriers to effective listening.

FIGURE SEVEN:
BARRIERS TO COMMUNICATION

PREOCCUPATION
LACK OF INTEREST
EXTERNAL NOISE
INTERNAL NOISE
MISUNDERSTANDING

PREOCCUPATION

A major barrier to listening is that of *preoccupation*. It is a matter of simply not concentrating on what is being communicated. Instead of listening to the intended message, we are giving our primary attention to some other communication source, or else we are concentrating on some other thought or daydream.

For example, have you ever tried to communicate with a husband who is watching Monday Night Football, or with a teenager who is listening to her stereo, or to a woman who is visiting with a friend on the telephone? Each of them is preoccupied with another communication source. Or have you tried to communicate with a student who is working on an algebra problem, or with a woman who is sewing, or with a young lady who is thinking about her next date? Each of them is preoccupied with another factor.

Often I have been working in my study when one of my three children has come to ask me permission to do something. Without breaking away from what I am doing to listen to them, I have simply nodded or grunted my approval. When I hear their squeal of delight, I usually come to my senses and begin to listen, now deeply interested in discovering what I have just given them permission to do.

Preoccupation negates the possibility of empathetic and comprehending listening!

LACK OF INTEREST

Another major barrier to effective listening is simply *lack of interest*. There is a large body of communications theory which deals with this. For example, there is what communication theorists call *selective exposure*, which reveals that we basically listen to only that in which we are interested. We learn to "tune out" what we do not care about and to "tune in" those things which interest us. Most of us have mastered this art in regard to our television viewing. We can watch a movie or sports event with great interest, but "tune out" the commercials, which we do not desire to see or hear. Teenagers often display great skill in "tuning out" conversation while at the same time "tuning in" such important events as dinnertime or snacktime.

Lack of interest can prevent us from listening to others with empathy and concern.

EXTERNAL NOISE

We have already discussed the existence and the characteristics of external noise in Chapter Three. However, it is important to understand that *external noise* is one of the five major barriers to effective listening.

As we have noted, external noise is usually manifested in the form of some physical barrier, such as sounds and sights which distract us and thus prevent authentic and productive listening.

When we find ourselves concentrating more on the external noise than on the source of the message being communicated, we can be sure that the listening process has been defeated.

INTERNAL NOISE

The fourth barrier to effective listening is *internal noise.* As we previously discussed, this barrier is far more difficult to recognize and to overcome than external noise.

Internal noise is basically a negative attitude or negative conduct barrier. In most situations, the problem is that we are so involved in our own lives and concerns, we simply do not give priority to listening to the needs or interests of others.

The greatest tragedy of internal noise as a barrier is that most of us do not recognize it in ourselves. It is relatively easy to observe it in others, but it is extremely difficult to spot it in our own lives. We tend to see the splinter in our brother's eye, but have difficulty in seeing the log in our own.

Internal noise is the most difficult listening barrier to recognize and to subsequently overcome!

MISUNDERSTANDING

The fifth and final category of listening barriers is that of *misunderstanding.* How many times we have been disappointed or hurt by misunderstanding.

As you will remember, verbal messages are external, but the meaning of those messages must be translated internally. Here lies our basic problem. Misunderstanding is an intentional or unintentional error in decoding or translating the meaning of a message.

All of us have experienced that kind of situation in which one person says to another, "That's what you said!" The reply comes, "I did *not* say that!" The exchange continues back and forth until the communicator finally protests, "Maybe that is what you heard me say, but that is not what I meant!"

Each of us has been equipped with a filter which often allows us to hear only what we want to hear. We become masters at "tuning out" what we don't want to hear. Some problems of misunderstanding come at this very point. If a teenager does not like to carry out the garbage, he may consciously or unconsciously "tune out" the message and thus misunderstand it.

Fortunately, however, most misunderstanding exists not by an intentional act of the listener's will, but authentically because of the mistranslation of the meaning of the message.

Misunderstanding, then, is a critical barrier to empathetic and comprehending listening.

OVERCOMING THE LISTENING BARRIERS

Although these five barriers present a great threat to effective communication, they can be overcome. In fact, each of those potential barriers can actually be transformed into conduit through which effective communication can flow. Those challenges can become friends rather than enemies to the communication process.

The key to the transformation from enemy to friend is *you*! By an act of your will and with some hard work and practical application, you can convert those barriers into channels of effective listening.

FIGURE EIGHT:
OVERCOMING COMMUNICATION BARRIERS

FEEDBACK · LOVE—OPENNESS · CLEAR AWAY BARRIERS · CARING · CONCENTRATION

CONCENTRATION

We must begin by substituting concentration for preoccupation. The key is being *available* and *attentive*. When someone is speaking to us, we need to lay aside all else and be totally available to the communicator. This requires concentration and commitment!

Then we need to follow up on our availability by being genuinely attentive. Listening demands exertion—it is work! But like any other skill, the more we practice it, the easier it becomes.

We have the innate capacity and ability to be good listeners. The average person speaks at the rate of approximately 125 words per minute. In contrast, we have been equipped to receive verbal communication at four times that rate! We must become available and then genuinely attentive in order to concentrate and thereby to listen effectively.

Concentration is the key to overcoming the barrier of preoccupation!

GENUINE INTEREST/CARING

Our next transformation needs to be the replacing of lack of interest with *genuine interest* and *caring*. We need to begin by focusing upon the source or the communicator. True listening requires that we become more concerned with the communicator than with the message. We need to care about the communicator as a person who has value.

For example, how often has a child whom you loved communicated an unimportant message in which you had little interest? Yet you listened to the message with great interest because you loved and cared for the child who was communicating it.

We need the same quality of love and care for everyone who communicates with us. What a difference when love takes the place of lack of interest!

Another focus needs to be that of *identification.* Authentic listening requires that we identify with the communicator—that there be a genuine "point of contact." We can actually identify with the communicator even if we totally disagree with his message!

In other words, it is extremely important that we meet people where they are. We need to rejoice with those who rejoice, and weep with those who weep! Identification means that I meet a person where he or she actually is, not where I think he or she should be.

For example, an attractive young bride recently

came to me for counseling. She and her sweetheart had been married for just a few months when he was killed in a tragic accident. Needless to say, she was filled with a great sense of loss and was experiencing deep grief.

However, her grief was not her major problem. Instead, her greater problem was her relatives and friends who were refusing to identify with her sorrow and instead were attempting to get her to "forget the past," "lift up your chin and be happy," and try to begin a new love relationship with someone else. She did not need that kind of counsel and encouragement. What she needed was someone to identify with her grief, to listen to her, and to offer comfort.

In summary, genuine interest, caring, and identification are the keys to overcoming the barrier of lack of interest.

CLEAR ALL EXTERNAL NOISE

External noise must be met head-on. In most cases it can be totally removed or at least substantially reduced. Each of us must assume personal responsibility for the noise that prevents effective communication. If we wait for someone else to remove the noise, we will usually have to wait too long a time.

The mutual removing of external noise barriers is often the best method. In other words, if you and the person with whom you are communicating will help one another remove the noise barrier, you will take a very long and positive step toward effective communication.

There are obvious exceptions to your responsibility. For example, if you are a guest in someone's home and they have a television set tuned on with the volume loud enough to prevent you from listening properly, you certainly do not have the responsibility to turn it down or off. To do so would be rude and out of place. However, you may gently suggest the possibility. At that time, it becomes your host's responsibility.

In short, you need to take the initiative in removing or reducing all physical barriers which fall into the realm of your responsibility!

LOVE AND OPENNESS

Next, the internal noise barriers need to be replaced with *love* and *openness*. Love is the most essential ingredient in maximum communication. In fact, we shall deal with the exciting subject of love in much more detail in Chapter Six.

However, we must point out now that genuine love is the primary solution in overcoming internal noise. For example, when you truly love your neighbor as yourself, you no longer feel superior or inferior. Your self-centeredness will melt away and become mutual-centeredness. You will still be concerned about yourself, but your concern will expand to include others. Love replaces the need to be dogmatic and judgmental. Love erases insensitivity. Love is sensitive to the needs, cares, and concerns of others. Love never manipulates, nor does it dominate. Compulsive speech is no longer needed.

Several years ago, a mother came to me expressing utter frustration. She simply could not communicate with her teenage daughter. Whenever she tried to speak to her, their conversation always ended in a vicious argument. She felt that unless her daughter was willing to change, she would have to place her in a foster home.

As I began to visit with the mother, I quickly discovered that she never talked *with* her daughter. Instead, she always talked *at* her. In other words, she took a very authoritarian, judgmental role in communicating with her daughter. Internal noise barriers made effective communication impossible.

As I counseled this mother on how to replace

those barriers with love and openness, she became very defensive. However, she finally agreed to try it for one week. When she returned for our next counseling session, I could tell that things were beginning to change in her relationship with her daughter.

As she began to reach out to her daughter with love and openness, an amazing thing happened. Her daughter began to respond with love and openness. During the succeeding weeks, their relationship was transformed from brokenness and bitterness to love, openness, and trust. Both mother and daughter became responsible and accountable for their own actions.

You cannot always remove the internal noise from others, but you can deal effectively with it in your own life. You can replace the negative attitude and conduct barriers in your own life with active love.

Love is the key in overcoming internal noise!

FEEDBACK

Misunderstanding can be transformed by the practice of *feedback*. As the term implies, feedback simply involves feeding the message back to the communicator in order to be certain that you have received it and translated it properly.

There are two primary methods for employing feedback effectively. The first is referred to as *parroting*. This is the act of repeating the message back to the communicator virtually word for word as you heard it. For example, if you believe the person said to you, "You have big feet," repeat those words back to him by saying, "I understand that you said that I have big feet."

This gives the communicator the opportunity to confirm or correct the message. He may reply, "I'm so sorry, but you misunderstood what I was saying. I actually said, Please take a seat!"

In such a situation, you can be grateful that you parroted the message. You both can enjoy a good laugh together, and then continue with your conversation. We obviously do not feed back with the parroting device with every sentence spoken. That would become a tremendous barrier in itself, and would actually cause effective communication to break down.

Feedback should only be used when you feel it to be necessary or helpful. Basically, it should take place when you feel that you might have misunderstood the communicator's message or when something is not clear to you.

The second major feedback device is called *paraphrasing*. This is the act of responding to the communicator by rephrasing his or her message in your own words. You may introduce your paraphrase by stating, "Is this what I hear you saying . . . ?" or "I believe that I may have misunderstood you. I thought you said . . . Is that correct?"

In other words, you are not accusing the person of making a given statement. You are simply restating what you thought you heard and are asking for a clarification. You may do this by simply saying, "What you say is very important to me, and I don't think that I understood what you have said. Would you please repeat it for me?"

Unfortunately, so many friendships and personal relationships have been broken or disrupted because someone did not take the initiative to employ feedback. Most misunderstandings can be resolved through this simple device.

Feedback is also effective when someone makes a statement in haste, frustration, or anger. Feedback gives the communicator an opportunity to regain his composure and to clarify what he was really trying to say.

Appropriate and sensitive feedback is a wonderful substitute for misunderstanding.

MASTERING LISTENING

Overcoming the various communication barriers is imperative if empathetic and comprehending listening is to take place. However, although this is a vital step in the communication process, it cannot stand alone.

Other vital factors are also necessary in order for maximum communication to take place. We are complex beings who are wonderfully made in the image of God. A part of our complexity is in our emotional makeup. If we are to become effective communicators, we must move on to the important consideration of mirroring feelings!

SUGGESTED EXERCISES TO HELP YOU MASTER LISTENING:

1. List and then analyze the basic listening barriers which you most often encounter in your life. Select the one barrier which seems to be the greatest challenge in your life. Then carefully plan a strategy to help you overcome the stated barrier. If possible, ask for the counsel of persons who are close to you who can share objective and positive input on how you can personally overcome the stated barrier.

2. Then begin to practice overcoming this barrier in your real life. You will be able to learn by doing—and even failing at times—just as a child learns to walk by falling and then trying again. Make notes of your experiences and progress. Don't give up! Keep practicing!

3. When you have made some significant progress with the first barrier, proceed with the same strategy to begin working on a second barrier. Follow the same basic procedure on the second and then the third until you have undertaken all five categories of barriers. However, don't try too much at once. Focus

on just one new barrier at a time, but continue to practice the previous assignments. Keep on keeping on!

4. Whenever possible, try to enlist one other person to join you in these exercises. You will find that you will be a great encouragement and help to one another. You will also become accountable to each other, which will encourage you to be faithful to the exercise rather than dropping out!

FIVE:
MIRRORING FEELINGS

KEY#4: *MIRROR FEELINGS. We must recognize and admit our feelings and then become sensitive in responding to the feelings of other persons.*

How often have you been asked, "How do you feel today?" Or how often have you expressed yourself by saying, "I feel just great!" or "I don't feel very well." We are constantly in the process of assessing and expressing our feelings. Yet if I were to ask you to define the term "feelings," you would probably have some difficulty in doing so.

In reality, feelings are merely the expression of your present state or condition. When you express your feelings, you are actually expressing the "real you" at a given moment. Feelings communicate the reality of the inner you. They reveal your inner condition.

When feelings are expressed, they communicate just as clearly as words or other forms of nonverbal communication such as body language or eye contact. We are constantly communicating to others through our feelings.

However, it is true that some people are more free to express their feelings than others. We often envy those people who are able to communicate freely through their feelings.

Unfortunately, one reason people indulge in alcohol or drugs is because they lose some of their inhibitions and are more free to communicate their feelings after use. In fact, if you have ever attended a cocktail party you have witnessed this dynamic. The party usually begins quietly and reservedly. However, after the guests have had a few drinks, the sound level rises markedly, and people become much more free and open in their expressions. Some become silly or giddy while others become obnoxious. In one sense, the real person is being expressed—and sometimes the "real you" is not very desirable.

That is a major reason why many people suppress their feelings. They do not like the real person inside of them, and they do not want to expose that inner person to others. So they become closed, detached, and often defensive.

I once met a brilliant man who was as cold and calculating as anyone I have ever known. Needless to say, he was also a very lonely person. As we were visiting together one evening, he became more warm and open in his relationship to me. Within that context, I said to him, "I sense that I have never met the real you. I believe that under that brilliant, calculating mind of yours is a very special person whom I would like to get to know better." He paused for some time and then said, "No, I would never like you to meet the real me, because if you did you certainly wouldn't like me." And with that, he closed the conversation and sadly walked away.

What is the answer to such a dilemma? How can we express our feelings with openness and freedom? How can we make our feelings our servants, and not our masters? How can we change our inner self so that we can express it with joy and excitement rather than with shame?

The last question will be answered in the final chapter of this book. However, we will proceed now to answer the questions regarding how we can communicate our feelings with openness and freedom as masters of a given situation.

YOU NEED TO UNDERSTAND YOUR OWN FEELINGS

We must begin by acknowledging the fact that feelings are an important reality in our lives. We have been created as emotional beings who have feelings. Many of us would gain a new dimension of freedom if we would only acknowledge the existence of our emotions.

The problem is that many of us have been taught since we were very young that we should not express our feelings. For example, many boys have been programmed to believe that men never cry. That simply is not true—and when we deny that fact, we are denying reality.

We need to acknowledge our feelings to ourselves. We may not like those feelings, but we can never deal with them until we admit their existence. Only then can we begin to deal with them and change them for the better!

For example, have you ever been angry at someone you love very deeply? Rather than expressing that anger, we often suppress it and become quiet. When that special person asks us what is wrong, we often reply by saying that we are simply not in the mood to talk. In truth, the problem can never be resolved until we acknowledge our feelings of anger, express them in a constructive way, and then deal with the problem.

Our lives tend to be like a river which is flowing gently and beautifully within the banks, with the flow under control, or like an angry, raging river that is flooded out of its banks, bringing destruction and death to all in its wake. What a difference your emotions can make when they are under control.

Once we have acknowledged the existence of feelings, the next step is to learn to recognize or identify them. Because many of us have suppressed feelings for so long, we often cannot identify how we are actually feeling.

A difficulty in identifying feelings adequately is that we are complex emotional beings, and there are so many ways we can feel. In the final pages of this chapter I have listed over 200 examples of feelings. No wonder we have difficulty in adequately understanding how we feel! However, this list should not discourage you! Most feelings fall into the general categories of good or bad, positive or negative, up or down.

For example, most negative feelings have to do with threat of hurt or loss. Most positive feelings have to do with success or contentment or hope. In most situations of life, you will be able to recognize why you feel the way you do. For example, if you have just experienced the death of a dear friend, it is very natural for you to experience grief. The sense of loss results in negative feelings.

Or if you have just won $100,000 in a contest, it is very appropriate for you to feel ecstatic and wonderful. In other words, the experiences of the real you determine your feelings. That is why people who have a negative image of themselves and their world never seem to feel good feelings. The focus of negative images results in negative feelings. This is a vicious circle!

If we are to communicate our own feelings adequately and then respond appropriately to the feelings of others, we must begin by acknowledging the reality of our feelings and then learn to recognize and identify them.

YOU NEED TO BE RESPONSIBLE FOR YOUR FEELINGS

As we learn to acknowledge and identify our feelings, we must also learn to assume responsibility for them. Feelings come from within. Only you are responsible for your feelings.

For example, a situation that makes one person cry may make another person laugh. Or what may make John angry may move Mary with deep compassion. Our lives are a complex composite of our past, our beliefs, and our temperaments which all influence our given situation. That is why we need to know ourselves and to assume responsibility for our own feelings.

Because of our human nature, we often attempt to assign the responsibility for our feelings at a given moment on someone else. For example, we may say, "She makes me mad!" or "He makes me sick!" That simply is not true. Other people do not cause us to become angry or sick; we *allow* others to influence us in that way.

Blaming your negative feelings on others is a cop-out. Another person may provide the stimuli for your negative feelings, but you have the ability to respond to that stimuli as you choose. You and you alone determine whether you are going to respond in anger or with humor. You are in charge of your feelings! You are responsible!

How freeing it is to assume responsibility for our own feelings. God has given each of us the ability to control our emotions. When your emotions control you, you are out of control. When you control your emotions, you are in control of your life!

YOU NEED TO EXPRESS YOUR FEELINGS POSITIVELY

When you are in control of your feelings, then you are in the wonderful position of being able to express them openly. Unfortunately, many of us have mastered the art of suppressing our feelings. Because our feelings are often negative and potentially destructive, we have felt the need to hold them down.

If you are constantly suppressing your emotions, you can be certain of one thing—you will become physically and/or emotionally and/or spiritually ill. Suppression leads to illness. In fact, some physicians suggest that up to 75 percent of physical illnesses are caused by psychosomatic sources. Suppressing your emotions will never bring you peace of mind or well-being. It may bring you to an experience of "blowing up" or of "breaking down," but it will never result in personal fulfillment.

I recently counseled a young man who had gone through a very painful breakup of his engagement. His beautiful fiancée had forsaken him for another. As a result, he had moved into a very deep state of depression. For months he had been counseled by both a psychologist and psychiatrist, but to no avail.

As we visited together, it became very apparent that his basic problem was one of frustration and anger. He simply would not forgive the young lady, and in not forgiving her he paid a terrible price. Only when he was able to forgive her and to allow God to forgive him was he set free from his terrible depression.

If you are to enjoy a life of openness and fulfillment, you must express your emotions. In fact, you can never actually understand or gain control of your emotions until you begin to be honest in expressing them.

As you begin to assume responsibility for your feelings and as you gain control over your emotions, you will learn to express your feelings in a positive, constructive way rather than using them as a destructive force. The so-called negative emotions can be controlled and channeled positively.

For example, anger is a very appropriate feeling in some situations. How wonderful it is to learn to express that anger with love in order to build a relationship rather than to destroy or harm it.

I have learned that anger is a very appropriate and constructive emotion when it is under proper control. But what a difference it makes when I express anger by exploding and hurting another person, either visibly or emotionally. When I attempt to express my anger appropriately through love, not by suppressing or denying my anger, but by expressing it in a constructive way, it will help the other person grow.

Let me share a very simple illustration of this principle. Suppose that Billy's mother had specifically asked him not to color pictures on his bedroom wall, and Billy had proceeded to disobey his mother. She could respond in at least two ways. She could become very angry, scream at Billy, and proceed to physically punish him. However, how much more helpful it would be for both Billy and his mother if she could express her anger to him verbally, express why she had not wanted him to draw pictures on his wall, and then proceed to correct him by allowing him to remove all of his artwork.

In other words, Billy needs to learn that he cannot control his mother or throw her out of control. Instead, he must always pay the consequences for his disobedient actions. Of course, at such times a spanking may also be in order. However, it is important for Billy to realize that the spanking is not a result of his mother's anger, but is a consequence of his disobedience.

Those same principles need to be transferred to our relationships with other adults. We need to recognize that no one else can "make us angry." We have the right to decide whether or not we become angry and whether (or how) that anger should be expressed.

We need to not suppress our feelings, but to express them honestly and constructively!

YOU NEED TO RESPOND TO THE FEELINGS OF OTHERS

As we are learning to recognize and to assume responsibility for our own feelings and then to express them openly and constructively, we are ready to learn to respond to the feelings of others. We must begin with our own lifestyle. As you communicate with others, practice being totally honest by expressing not just facts or information, but also your feelings.

As you practice this openness in your own life, you will be encouraging others to do the same. Only when you become responsible for your own feelings will you be able to become effective in responding to the feelings of others.

Identification becomes a very important tool. As people are communicating to you verbally, try to identify not only with what they are saying, but with the communicator as a person. Listen not only to the verbal message, but be attentive to the feelings being expressed.

Then attempt to "mirror" those feelings as you respond to the person. Respond to the communicator where he is—not where you would like him to be. Don't fall into the trap of trying to psychoanalyze the communicator. Simply respond to him as he is and where he is with love and sensitivity. In short, we need to learn to rejoice with those who rejoice and to weep with those who are weeping. If we are to become effective communicators, we need to become all things to all persons according to their need.

Maximum communication includes my willingness to be available to identify with another person and to respond with genuine concern and with practical help.

In mirroring emotions, we need to care, share, encourage, identify, build up, bear burdens, respond to hurts, bring healing, and bind wounds—all with feelings of compassion and authentic love!

HOW CAN I DO THE IMPOSSIBLE?

The question then becomes, How do I pull that off? Again I must ask for your patience in awaiting the "how to" of the last chapter. However, the key to this kind of openness and maximum communication begins with love. Let's move on to the key of love!

SUGGESTED EXERCISES TO HELP YOU MIRROR FEELINGS:

1. Read the list of potential feelings found on pages 64-65. Try to identify personally with each feeling. Think back to specific instances in your life when you experienced that particular feeling. Circle those words you can identify as ones you have experienced frequently in your life. Then underline those which you have only experienced infrequently. Finally, place a check mark in front of those which you never remember experiencing or which you simply do not understand.

2. Share your analysis with someone who is close to you. Attempt to discover together why you have not been able to identify with certain feelings. What, if anything, seems to prevent you from such experiences?

3. Attempt to log your feelings for the next three days. Carry a notebook with you and attempt to record your feelings just as accurately as possible. Attempt to identify not only *what* you are feeling, but *why* you are feeling a certain way. Have the person who is close to you help you in attempting to experience feelings which are new to you. At the end of the three days, share your experiences and discoveries together. Then repeat the exercise as needed until you are free to feel and you are able to identify your feelings and to express them constructively.

4.   When you become more aware of your own feelings, begin to practice listening to the feelings of other people. Attempt not to "react" to those feelings or simply to "analyze" them. Instead, respond to them with love and sensitivity. Learn to meet people where they are— not where you assume them to be or would desire them to be! Mirror the feelings of others!

EXAMPLES OF FEELINGS

ABANDONED
ADAMANT
ADEQUATE
AFFECTIONATE
AGONY
ALMIGHTY
AMBIVALENT
ANGRY
ANNOYED
ANXIOUS
APATHETIC
ASTOUNDED
AWED

BAD
BEAUTIFUL
BETRAYED
BITTER
BLISSFUL
BOLD
BORED
BRAVE
BURDENED

CALM
CAPABLE
CAPTIVATED
CHALLENGED
CHARMED
CHEATED
CHEERFUL
CHILDISH
CLEVER
COMBATIVE
COMPETITIVE
CONDEMNED
CONFUSED
CONSPICUOUS

CONTENTED
CONTRITE
CRUEL
CRUSHED
CULPABLE

DECEITFUL
DEFEATED
DELIGHTED
DESIROUS
DESPAIRING
DESTRUCTIVE
DETERMINED
DIFFERENT
DIFFIDENT
DIMINISHED
DISCONTENTED
DISTRACTED
DISTRAUGHT
DISTURBED
DOMINATED
DIVIDED
DUBIOUS

EAGER
ECSTATIC
ELECTRIFIED
EMPTY
ENCHANTED
ENERGETIC
ENERVATED
ENJOYING
ENRAGED
ENVIOUS
EVIL
EXASPERATED
EXCITED
EXHAUSTED

FASCINATED
FAWNING
FEARFUL
FLUSTERED
FOOLISH
FRANTIC
FREE
FRIGHTENED
FRUSTRATED
FULL
FURIOUS

GAY
GLAD
GOOD
GRATIFIED
GREEDY
GRIEVING
GROOVY
GUILTY
GULLIBLE

HAPPY
HATEFUL
HEAVENLY
HELPFUL
HELPLESS
HIGH
HOMESICK
HONORED
HORRIBLE
HURT
HYSTERICAL

IGNORED
IMMORTAL
IMPOSED UPON
IMPRESSED

INFATUATED
INFURIATED
INSPIRED
INTIMIDATED
ISOLATED

JEALOUS
JOYOUS
JUMPY

KIND
KEEN

LAZY
LECHEROUS
LEFT OUT
LICENTIOUS
LONELY
LONGING
LOVING
LOW
LUSTFUL

MAD
MAUDLIN
MEAN
MELANCHOLY
MISERABLE
MYSTICAL

NAUGHTY
NERVOUS
NICE
NUTTY

OBNOXIOUS
OBSESSED
ODD
OPPOSED
OUTRAGED
OVERWHELMED

PAINFUL

PANICKED
PARSIMONIOUS
PEACEFUL
PERSECUTED
PETRIFIED
PITY
PLEASANT
PLEASED
PRECARIOUS
PRESSURED
PRETTY
PRIM
PRISSY
PROUD

QUARRELSOME
QUEER

RAPTUROUS
REFRESHED
REJECTED
RELAXED
RELIEVED
REMORSEFUL
RESTLESS
REVERENT
REWARDED
RIGHTEOUS

SAD
SATED
SATISFIED
SCARED
SERVILE
SETTLED
SHOCKED
SILLY
SKEPTICAL
SNEAKY
SOLEMN
SORROWFUL

SPITEFUL
STARTLED
STINGY
STRANGLED
STUFFED
STUPID
STUNNED
STUPEFIED
SUFFERING
SURE
SYMPATHETIC

TALKATIVE
TEMPTED
TENACIOUS
TENSE
TENTATIVE
TENUOUS
TERRIBLE
TERRIFIED
THREATENED
THWARTED
TIRED
TRAPPED
TROUBLED

UGLY
UNEASY
UNSETTLED

VEHEMENT
VIOLENT
VITAL
VIVACIOUS
VULNERABLE

WEEPY
WICKED
WONDERFUL
WORRIED

ZANY

SIX:
UNDERSTANDING AND PRACTICING LOVE

KEY#5: *UNDERSTAND AND PRACTICE LOVE. We must understand the dynamics of love and then actively practice the lifestyle of love!*

The romanticists have long contended that only love can make the world go round. And as far as human communication is concerned, they are absolutely correct! Authentic love is the most essential and important factor involved in the personal communication process. Love is the key to effective and meaningful human relationships.

Without love, interpersonal communication is merely mechanical. Love is to communication what the bloodstream is to the human body. Without the flow of blood to its cells, the human body becomes a mere corpse. And without love being central to our personal communication, relationships with others will become ultimately dead. Love brings life!

LOVE AS NEED

Only love can meet a primary need of mankind. If behavioral scientists agree on any common tenet, it is that a universal need of all persons is the need to be loved—and to love! No human need is more apparent in our daily lives than the need for love.

In fact, much of our personal behavior is an expression of our basic need to be loved. We desire to be recognized, appreciated, and affirmed. And we usually behave in such a manner that we are inviting the response of love.

All of us have observed children who are showing off in a sincere attempt to receive attention and to win approval. Much of our adult behavior is merely a veiled expression of that same mode of behavior—which is seeking for a loving and affirming response.

Advertisers use the mass media to meet us at this precise point of need, and subsequently they attempt to motivate us to buy their particular product in order for that need to be met. We are constantly being barraged with newspaper ads or radio and television spots which assure us that given products such as deodorant, mouthwash, or even an automobile will make us more accepted and loved.

Many of us have tried such products with great expectations—and have been sorely disappointed with the actual results. We have discovered that the scent of a certain shaving lotion or the shade of a given lipstick is not the crucial key to enjoying love and acceptance. Enjoying the love of others and living the life of love demands more than that. Authentic love is much more expensive!

LOVE IS EXPENSIVE

The worth of love cannot be measured in dollars, pounds, or even gold. Nor can love be measured in the terms of power, influence, or prestige. Love must ultimately be weighed on the scale of human and eternal values.

Love is always *expensive*. It can never be purchased at a discount; it is never on sale. The price tags on authentic love are remarkably high. However, it is equally available to the rich and the poor, the king and the beggar.

In other words, if you are to enjoy the life of love, there are some inescapable requirements which you must meet. Love does not merely flow down from some indefinable source. True love always comes from God. He is the only source of love.

Our final chapter will explore that important truth in more detail. However, for now we shall identify some of the price tags found on that wonderful commodity of love.

RISK

Love demands *risk*. You can never enjoy the life of love without taking some personal risks. In fact, every time you reach out to express love to another person, risk is involved. That person has the freedom of the will, either to respond to your love or to reject it. That is why your love must be unconditional. You must be willing to love even when you are unloved or rejected.

Without a doubt this is one of the greatest challenges of the life of love. I have met many people who have reached out to love another person, have been rejected, and have then retreated to the safety of their own personal being. They continue to live their lives as islands. They will not risk once again to love. Unfortunately they are the greatest losers. They have deprived themselves of life's very best—the life of love!

A sickly, frail young lady once came to me for counseling. Her story is one I have heard again and again. She had been deeply in love with a young man, had experienced a period of great joy in sharing life with him, and was then rejected by her sweetheart. She tried in vain to win back his love and attention. When he finally married another young lady, my counselee retreated to a loveless, bitter, empty life. She determined that she would never try to love again.

As a result, she was soon confined to a mental institution. She went through several years of psychiatric therapy, but she remained alone and withdrawn. Only when she committed her life to the God of love and began to reach out in love to others was she set free from her plight. Through God's love and through expressing that love to others, she was set free!

Authentic love stands regardless of the response. To be sure, you cannot enjoy the loving relationship of another without the mutual response of sharing love. But even when others reject your love, you can keep the door of your life open to them as you offer love with no strings attached.

All of us need to be on guard against the pitfall of allowing rejection to prevent us from enjoying the life of love. Many persons have reached out to love another, have been rejected, and then have retreated to a refuge of self-pity, defensiveness, and emptiness. In short, they are saying, "I tried to love and have been rejected. Therefore, I will never try to love again."

What a tragedy! They have allowed another person to rule their lives. They have retreated to a loveless existence simply because of one or even several experiences of rejection. How foolish it would be for a child to refuse to learn to walk simply because she fell a few times during the learning process. And how foolish it is to drop out of the wonderful life of love because of a few falls and bruises.

PAIN

To be sure, rejection is *painful*. I have often thought about the love of Jesus Christ in regard to rejection. Never has a human being loved so openly and authentically. And yet, crucified by men, forsaken by Father and Spirit, never has a person been so rejected!

The life of love does not excuse us from the pain of rejection. But the benefits far outweigh the pain. A single human relationship of sharing love is far greater than any pain which comes from rejection. Without a doubt, love is the greatest of all human experiences!

But love also demands the pain of inconvenience and personal identification. When you love another person, you are touched by her problems, questions, and hurts. Love celebrates when others celebrate and grieves when others grieve. Love shares *all*—even pain!

TIME

Love also requires *time.* This is a vital part of the inconvenience of love. You simply cannot love another only on your schedule. You must be willing to be available when the other needs you. Availability is an essential ingredient of authentic love.

Lust and self-centeredness are concerned about doing one's own thing at his time and in his way and at his desire. Love is available all the time; it keeps no office hours. Love is willing to be inconvenienced!

But that does not mean that love is to be taken advantage of by another. Love does not always say "yes!" Love must also say "no!"

DECISION

Love requires important *decisions*—and these decisions are often difficult. For example, there is the situation of a person whom we love asking for something which we believe will hurt him rather than help him. Love cannot say "yes" to that kind of request. Convenience may say "yes," but love cannot! Loving parents would not give their children poison, and loving persons do not give to others that which would bring them harm or destruction. Love must sometimes say "no."

However significant or insignificant the decision may be, love should be our basic criterion. The basic question which we need to pose as we are facing decisions is, "Will the results of this decision be good for me and for those I love? Will others be helped or hurt by this decision?"

Love must often be tough and firm. It cannot compromise regarding what is right and just. Love must always build and never tear down. Love makes the right decisions!

SENSITIVITY

Such decisions and such actions require a great deal of *sensitivity*. Sensitivity is to love what an antenna is to a television set. Accurate reception and appropriate responses are dependent upon authentic sensitivity. If you are to actually love another person, you must begin by being sensitive to that person's needs. Only then can you respond in love by offering practical solutions to those needs.

For example, if a person comes to you who is starving, it is not appropriate to merely pat him on the head and wish him God's best. The only appropriate initial response is to give him food and nourishment.

Or, as I mentioned earlier in the book, if a person comes to you who is grieving, love will not allow you to ignore those feelings of hurt or loss. Instead, love would require a sensitive identification with those feelings of grief.

Sensitivity is a matter of attention and focus. By nature, we are sensitive to our own needs. We know when we hurt or have specific needs. Love requires that we develop that same quality of sensitivity to the needs of others. Love has an antenna that is tuned in to the needs of others.

Unfortunately, such sensitivity is not an inherent trait. It must be learned. For most of us, sensitivity is not easy for us to master. While it seems to be more readily learned by some than others, sensitivity can become a part of all our lives. However, sensitivity is an art to be mastered only when we are willing to apply ourselves with a deep commitment.

You can become a truly sensitive person only when you allow love to be your basic motive. If you want to develop the important quality of sensitivity, you must desire to have it and must actively practice it. And that kind of practice and experience begins with our motives.

LOVE AS MOTIVE

Authentic love must always begin with motive. Motive is the key to our human conduct. If you wish to outwardly express love in action, that love must originate within your inner being. In reality, love as conduct proceeds from the heart.

In other words, a person's behavior is determined by his inner motive. The word motive comes from the Latin word *motum*, which literally means "to move." Motive is that which induces action or causes motion!

If love becomes your primary inner motive, your life will begin to be characterized by the lifestyle of love! This quality of love is quite different from that which is merely an outward facade. Fabricated love is shallow and undependable. Its existence is like a stage actor who is going through the motions, but simply does not have the authentic goods.

Love that is genuine must flow from the inner heart. It cannot be fabricated. Such love begins with motive, and then manifests itself with authentic expression in word and deed. If this is so, what are the actual characteristics of genuine love?

CHARACTERISTICS OF LOVE

In order to better understand love, we must identify the basic ingredients.

Love is very *patient*. By nature, most of us are impatient. In fact, some of us have mistaken laziness for patience. However, authentic patience is active—not passive. Love is patient, and it equips us to become patient.

By nature, I want everything to take place *now*. However, I have found that when I actively love another person, I become much more patient with his or her actions which would normally perturb me.

I have a friend who speaks very slowly and deliberately. I used to attempt to "speed him up" by interrupting his sentence and completing it for him. However, love helped me to recognize that I was not helping him. To the contrary, my interruptions were frustrating and even hurting him. Love encouraged me to be still and to listen and to wait for him to express himself. Love is patient!

The next time you tend to become impatient with another person, attempt to substitute love for your impatience. What a difference you will experience!

Love is also *kind*. When we love a person, it is obvious that we relate to her with kindness. Most of us have been taught since we were young children to be kind to animals or to the disadvantaged or handicapped person. While this is commendable, love is kind to *every* person who comes into our lives—rich or poor, black or white, male or female, good or evil. Love is always kind!

Love is *not envious or jealous*. Love identifies with the needs of others. It can rejoice with those who are rejoicing and weep with those who are weeping. It never attempts to be "one-up!" Love never communicates feelings of superiority or inferiority. It meets people on the level—eyeball to eyeball.

There is *no pretense* in love. It can always be honest and open. Love is transparent. It does not merely pretend not to be envious or jealous. To the contrary, love genuinely rejoices with the successes and joys of others. It does not need to take from others in order to be satisfied. Love realizes that the grass is not always greener on the other side of the fence. Love relates to reality.

One of the great joys of the life of love is the ability to rejoice with other people's successes. To be sure, all of us enjoy a certain measure of personal success and achievement. But how it is compounded when we rejoice in the successes and achievements of others whom we love! "Loving our neighbor as we love ourselves" multiplies our joy many times!

Love is *not boastful or arrogant or rude.* Love is the very essence of human fulfillment and security, and so it eliminates the need to boast.

Love does not need to be arrogant or rude. It is always concerned with what is best not only for self, but for others. It recognizes that what is best for self and what is best for others are not mutually exclusive. Instead, they are in harmony with each other. When love is present, what is best for one is best for the other.

Of course this kind of statement is based upon the assumption that life is not merely an accident, but that God really is in control of the universe and is concerned about all of our lives. I have discovered that when God blesses me, it is never to the detriment of someone else. God's blessing is not directed toward me in isolation, but has the potential of being a mutual blessing for others involved in my life. When someone else gets a promotion and I do not, I can still authentically rejoice, because as I love that other person his blessing becomes my blessing.

This is one of the basic distinctions between love and lust. Lust always demands and takes for its own gratification with little or no concern for the other. Love has a healthy concern for self and for others. It prefers to give and to share for the mutual welfare of all who are involved!

Love is *never touchy, irritable, or resentful.* Those qualities come from the roots of weakness, insecurity, or discontent. We may blame touchiness or irritability on our physical or emotional weariness. And we tend to blame resentment on our being abused or taken advantage of.

But love can be at full strength even when our bodies are weary or when we have been taken advantage of by other persons. Our daughter has suffered from a physical handicap since the age of one. As a result of her situation, we have spent a great deal of time with handicapped children. We have discovered that God has given Debbie and other handicapped children a very special capacity to love and be loved. If you ever spend any time around the mentally retarded, there too you will discover an incredible capacity for love.

There is nothing that love cannot face! We must be sure to understand that love is not weak, anemic, or wishy-washy. To the contrary, love is *strong!*

Love never delights in injustice, but rather *delights in the truth.* Love only settles for the right and the just—regardless of the cost. In fact, we have already explored together the fact of love being very expensive. The search for justice and truth is always very costly—and love leads the way. The Bible speaks very clearly about "speaking the truth in love." There is a way of expressing truth which is cutting and hurting and destructive. But when truth is expressed in love, it is constructive; it builds and encourages. Wherever there is truth and justice, there needs to be love!

Love is also *hopeful* and *optimistic.* This is a hope and optimism which is grounded in reality!

As we have discovered, love is capable of bringing life to relationships which are dead and alienated. And love has the potential to bring life to persons who have become empty and self-centered!

Many marriages which have died and have become hopeless situations could come alive and be filled with hope if love were to flow again within the dying relationship. Love can transform broken relationships between parents and children, husbands and wives, and employers and employees. In fact, I have never seen broken human relationships mended without the primary ingredient of love. The biblical story of the prodigal son stirs memories in most of our minds regarding similar situations in our own families or among our friends. Love has the potential of mending every broken human relationship. No wonder love is always hopeful and optimistic!

Love can literally overcome any obstacle. Love can endure anything and everything. Love is one of the few qualities of life which has the potential to live on forever! Authentic love never ends—and never fails!

LOVE AS COMMUNICATION

If all these things we have said about love are true, the legitimate question then becomes, "How do I live and communicate that kind of love? It sounds good in theory, but how do I pull it off?"

Those are excellent questions, and I will try to answer them in the next two chapters. I agree with you that we must do much more than merely understand what love is and what it costs. We need to understand how we can practice this quality of love within a practical lifestyle.

Let us begin by exploring together the highest form of human communication—dialog. Love is the key to authentic dialog, and dialog is the key to effective communication!

SUGGESTED EXERCISES FOR
UNDERSTANDING AND PRACTICING LOVE:

1. For seven consecutive days, read the sections
    in this chapter dealing with the characteris-
    tics of love. Then take a daily inventory of
    how you see these characteristics expressed
    in your life or through the lives of others.

2. At the end of each day, take a few moments to
    analyze your love inventory. Determine what
    specific expressions of love are being neglect-
    ed in your own life. Then commit yourself to
    begin to practice those characteristics in your
    life and in your world.

3. Give special attention to making love your
    motive. As you relate to people day by day,
    ask yourself, "Why am I relating in this way?
    What is my motive?"

4. Whenever possible, make love the motive for
    your conduct. Begin by focusing upon one or
    two persons who are especially near to you. In
    all that you do, attempt to make love your
    motive as you relate to them. Then broaden
    your circle to include more and more people.
    With practice and God's help, you can make
    love your motive!

SEVEN:
NOURISHING DIALOG

KEY #6: *NOURISH DIALOG. We must learn to nourish and then live the miracle of dialog.*

We began this book with a traditional definition and model of communication which we termed the "conveyor belt" theory. Although this is not the ultimate definition of communication, it was helpful in teaching us the basic components of the communication process.

As you know, we must learn to sit up before we crawl and to crawl before we walk. The "conveyor belt" theory helped us to sit up, and now a contemporary definition will help us learn to crawl. Then we will be prepared to walk!

A good contemporary definition of communication would be: Communication is the process of encounter. The model of the contemporary definition of communication is seen on the following page.

The key word for this model is *encounter*. This is actually an existential model which acknowledges that John and Mary are more than mere communicating objects. They are persons. And as persons they have both needs and anxieties. Communication in this model is much more than one commu-

FIGURE 9:

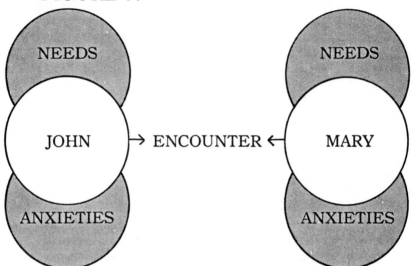

nicator (the source) dumping a load of information upon another (the destination). This model recognizes two individuals who have personal needs and anxieties and who reach out to each other in order to experience a meaningful encounter.

Although our personal needs vary from one person to another, all of us have needs. Behavioral scientists have suggested that there are several common needs which all of us possess, such as the need to love and the need to be loved. We also share the need to relate and communicate with others.

Then, of course, there are many specific needs which each one of us faces. Because we are dynamic beings, many of those needs change from day to day as we live out our lives.

Human beings also face the common reality of experiencing anxieties. It is often difficult for us to express needs or anxieties outwardly because we tend to feel that such expressions denote weakness or immaturity. However, until we recognize and acknowledge our needs and anxieties we will have little opportunity to grow or mature in those areas of our lives.

Some of the anxieties which are common to all of us include our fear of being unloved, of being rejected, of being alone, or of failing. Once again, we also experience specific personal anxieties which are basically the result of our past experiences or our present expectations.

When two persons acknowledge the existence of personal needs and anxieties, they can communicate on an entirely different level than they could otherwise. They have the potential of experiencing an authentic encounter. They are able to express honest and open feelings, to respond to each other with compassionate understanding, and to begin being transparent with each other. Encounter is a far cry from merely passing information from one object to another.

But there is an even higher level of communication. It is the *miracle of dialog*. Authentic dialog is communication in its highest and most meaningful form. A dialogical definition of communication is as follows: Communication is the process of creating relationship—to make common. It states, "I want to openly share my life with you. I will not only share my knowledge, strengths, and successes, but I will also be free to share my failings, questions, and needs. I will share my love and my feelings with you openly and honestly for our mutual benefit and growth."

The key word of dialogical communication is *love*! The model of dialogical communication is seen on the next page.

At first glance, the model seems to be almost identical to that of contemporary communication. Dialogical communication too is concerned with understanding that both the source and destination of the communication process are persons who have personal needs and anxieties. In fact, dialogical communication is concerned with all of

FIGURE 10:

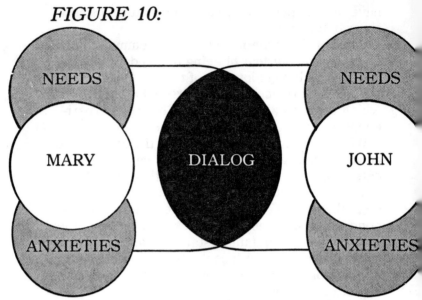

the dynamics revealed in the contemporary model, but dialog requires one additional giant step. It is the graduation from crawling to walking.

Dialog involves the act of sharing life. As you can see by the model, in dialogical communication John and Mary do not merely reach out for an encounter by sharing information or ideas; they actually reach out with their very lives. Dialogical communication takes place within the shared areas of their lives.

To be sure, they do not share their total lives. In fact, most of their lives remain personal and private. But by an overt act of their wills, they do share a portion of themselves with one another. This is dialog!

As an active dialogical relationship grows, the circle of dialog grows larger and larger. As they share life together, there is a growing of love, trust, and personal relationship. As the circle of dialog becomes larger, the circle of privacy and personal life becomes smaller. The ultimate dialogical relationship would be the total sharing of two lives one with another. It is intriguing to note that this is the biblical model for the marriage relationship—that two lives should become one!

In my opinion, this truth is the greatest refutation of so-called "trial marriages." Trial marriages can never be authentic. Only when two people make a covenant with each other and with God can the potential take place for the two lives to become one! That kind of total commitment and focus is absolutely essential for marriage. Indeed, such a relationship of love and trust and commitment is the epitome of the life of dialog.

However, please understand that the value of dialogical communication is not based upon the ultimate model of the total sharing of two lives. I believe that we need to live in some degree of dialogical relationship with every person who comes into our lives.

We do not need to share our total lives with another in order to enjoy the miracle of dialog. In fact, it is not wise or even possible to share large segments of our lives with everybody. The question arises, "How much of our lives should we share with another person, and how shall we determine the extent of our dialogical relationship?"

I can respond best to that important question by sharing a graphic model with you which depicts the options we have in determining our communications lifestyle. The model is presented on pages 84-85.

As you can see, the model is based upon the analogy of our lives being represented by a door. It is very important to understand that the model applies to *your* life and not that of another person. You are responsible for you, and I am not responsible for me! We are not responsible for another person's decision to open or not to open the door of their lives to us, but we are totally responsible as to whether or not we open our lives to others.

The area below the line represents the closed-

FIGURE 11:
DIALOGICAL COMMUNICATION

GROWING

OPEN DOOR
(Meaningful communication)

6. "INVITE IN!"

DIALOG:
Trust, shared life, love, sensitivity, *koinonia*, relationship, COMMUNION!

5. "OPEN DOOR"

ENCOUNTER:
Express honest feelings, open level, understanding!

4. "CRACK"

INFORMATION:
Fact-finding, becoming acquainted—who, what, where, when, why, how?

CLOSED DOOR
(Little or no communication)

3. "NO ONE IS HOME!"

DECEIVE:
Mislead, role play, air of superiority, insensitivity.

2. "NOT WELCOME!"

ATTACK:
Criticize, scold, dogmatic, give advice, condemn, tension, anger.

1. "LOCKED DOOR!"

IGNORE:
Withdraw, prejudge; apathetic, closed mind.

DYING

door policy of our lives. The CLOSED DOOR area is where there is little or no communication taking place. The negatives of internal noise dominate our relationships and prevent us from sharing or dialoguing with another. These three levels of communication ultimately lead to death. They represent dying relationships in various forms.

Locked Door: The first area is designated as "locked door." The key word is *ignore.* In other words, on this level of communication we choose to lock the door of our lives to a person and totally ignore him. If we were to give this area a temperature, it would be *cold.* We sometimes use the terminology of giving another person the "cold shoulder."

Have you ever encountered a person who "locked the door" of his life to you? I remember such a person in my own life. He literally would walk on the other side of the street to avoid me. If by chance I happened to be in a group of people with him, he would carry on the conversation as though I were not there. He would never look at me or talk to me. If I spoke to him or asked him a question, he would not respond. Needless to say, we did not experience mutual communication.

Other descriptive terms relating to the "Locked Door" level of communication would be to withdraw, prejudge, or to have a closed mind. As we can readily see, these are some of the sins of internal noise. When they dominate a personal relationship, there is death and dying!

Not Welcome: The second level of communication is not in any way superior to the first. It is merely another expression of the closed-door posture. This analogy is that of a person opening the door of their lives for a brief moment, seeing who is there, stating very clearly that the person is not welcome, and then slamming the door in his or her face. The key word is *attack!*

My first encounter with this level of communication is one that I experienced in junior high. I met a teacher whom I did not know in a school hallway. He came directly to me and began to attack me with verbal accusations, cursings, and scoldings. I was so startled and frightened that I literally ran away. I later discovered that he had mistaken me for another student. I will never forget the lack of communication in that particular encounter.

If we were to give this level a temperature, it would be *hot*. The "not welcome" syndrome is lived out in the form of criticizing, scolding, condemning, or being dogmatic. All of these expressions of the closed-door level of communication are expressions of external noise in its most vicious and insensitive forms.

No One Is Home: The third level of the closed-door area of communication is the most difficult to discern since the key word is *deceive!* This is the situation where someone comes to knock on the door of your life and you pretend that you do not hear them or that no one is home!

A number of years ago, while serving as pastor of a church, I attempted to visit the home of one of our members. As I approached the front door, I saw someone peek through the curtain of a window. Then I heard a disconcerting message uttered in a loud stage whisper. "Everybody be quiet! The pastor is here and the house is in a mess!"

I knew the people were home and they certainly knew they were home, but because they felt their house was unpresentable, they played the "no one is at home" game. As a result, no communication was able to take place.

The temperature of this elusive communication level would be *cool*. This closed-door lifestyle would be lived out through the use of the external noises of misleading, role playing, exhibiting an air of superiority, or being insensitive. Deception always leads to broken relationships, hurt, and ultimately the death of a relationship.

The three closed-door levels of communication are not even options to the person who is sincerely interested in effective communication. Maximum communication leads to growth and wholeness and fulfillment. Closed door communication results in decay, fragmentation, emptiness, and death!

But we do not need to live below the line. We can enjoy dialogical communication by practicing the open-door policy. As you can see in the model, the three levels of communication above the line are progressive and lead to growth and life at its best!

A Crack: Level 4 of the dialogical model encourages us to open the door of our lives at least a *crack* to everyone. The key word is *information.* This communication level involves us in the delightful act of becoming acquainted with another person by opening our lives to them through sharing basic information about ourselves. In turn, we invite them to do the same with us. The relevant ingredients of conversations on this level deal with the who, what, where, when, why, and how of our lives.

Probably the most helpful model of this level of communication would be the first model we shared (page 80). However, even this level of communication needs to move beyond the conveyor belt experience of merely dumping information upon one another. Hopefully there would be the beginning of a mutual exchange and sharing of life.

This level of opening the door of lives a crack to others and becoming acquainted is extremely important. It is impossible to authentically love another person without knowing her. To know her is the first step in loving her.

This fact is one of the basic differences between infatuation and authentic love. Infatuation may be satisfied with dreams and fantasies, but love always requires information and knowledge. The songwriter expressed it well when he said, "To know you is to love you—and I do!"

Open Door: The next level is a natural progression from opening the door a crack. If, for example, someone knocks on the door of your house, it is wise to open the door a crack to see who is there. When you are satisfied that the person who knocked is someone you know and can trust, your next step is usually that of opening the door!

That same progression should be followed in opening the door of our lives to other persons. (There are a few people we meet whom we cannot trust enough to open the door of our lives more than a crack. However, most people will merit the opening of lives in order to share more openly with them.)

The key word describing this level of communication would be *encounter*. At this level, we can begin to express our feelings honestly and openly. We can share some of our needs and concerns and can be responsive and understanding toward the needs expressed by the other person. In short, we can level with one another by expressing our authentic selves.

I find that as I open the door of my life a crack to other people, the natural result in most of my relationships is an encounter. Of course, sharing an encounter requires the involvement of both persons. It is impossible for you to encounter another who is not willing to respond in kind. This is a part of the level of risk which we spoke about earlier. We can reach out to others in love, but we can only enjoy an encounter if they respond.

If you are to enjoy the lifestyle of maximum communication, you must allow nearly all of your interpersonal relationships to proceed to this level of communication. Only for very specific reasons should you prevent another person from enjoying an open-door relationship with your life. Examples of such reasons would include your own physical safety or your emotional well-being. Again, we need to be reminded that you are responsible for you, and you must determine into what areas of your life you will invite other persons for dialogical communication.

Invite In: The third and highest level of open-door communication would be that of inviting another person into a specific area of your life for dialogical sharing. Once again, the analogy is quite graphic. Usually when a person knocks on your door, you open the door just a crack. When you are secure and can trust the person sufficiently, you then open the door. When your trust level becomes even deeper, you then feel free to invite the person into your house.

However, it is important to realize that when you invite a person into your life for dialogical communication, you do not invite him or her into your total life. You begin by inviting them into the foyer or living room. For many of your personal relationships, that will be as deep or as extensive as your relationship will ever be.

Other relationships will grow so that you will desire to invite that person into the dining room and/or other rooms of your life. You must always remember that only you can invite people into your life. However, each one of them must then decide whether or not he will respond—and whether mutually he will invite you to share in some of his life!

The greatest joys in my own human relationships have been when I have invited others into my life and they have come. It has been mutually beneficial when I have been invited into the lives of others and have responded to them. The life of dialog is the life of sharing. The more you love and invite others to share in your love, the more love will be shared with you. Love results in more love!

Remember, too, that you cannot force your way

into the life of someone else. You must be invited. You can knock, and you can suggest, and you can even ask, but you cannot enter unless you are invited.

Without a doubt, that is one of the most painful experiences of life—to open your life to another person but for that invitation not to be reciprocated. That is rejection in its most painful form.

As we previously discussed, authentic love always requires risk. There is risk involved when you reach out in love to another person and invite them to share a portion of life with you in dialogical communication. But as we have seen, authentic love is unconditional. It is more concerned with the other than with self. This reality is a major key to living and enjoying the life of dialog.

When we invite another person into our lives, we need to be sensitive regarding what rooms or areas of life are to be shared. I believe that there are some areas of intimacy in my life which are available only to my wife. There are other special and personal areas which are open to my children, and there are other areas open to my special friends. However, there are some rooms—even most rooms—which are open to everyone who wishes to share the life of dialog with me.

DIALOG AS LIFESTYLE

Dialog cannot be something we merely believe; it must become our very lifestyle! It cannot be an external; it must be woven into the very fabric of our lives. As you will notice, that is the focus of the sixth key of communication—we must learn to nourish and then to live the miracle of dialog!

Dialog, as we have defined it, is the ultimate communication experience. Most of us have had at least a little taste of what it is like. We desire the life of dialog and love and listening, but we aren't sure that we can actually achieve those attractive qualities. Our spirits have become excited about the possibilities, but our actual conduct seems to be lagging behind.

In fact, within most of us there seems to be a great gulf between what we want to be and what we actually are. We need another key—one that will not only tell us what we should do, but one that will enable us to do it. And that is exactly what the seventh key is all about!

SUGGESTED EXERCISES FOR LEARNING TO LIVE THE LIFE OF DIALOG:

1. Focus on one person with whom you can share on a deeper, more open, trusting level. Begin with your spouse, a member of your family, or a personal friend. Determine your present level of communication with this person. If it is below level 4, resolve any barriers that would prevent you from moving to level 4. Then attempt to progress from level 4 to 5 to 6—the life of dialogical communication.

2. As soon as possible, begin on level 4 with a newer friend whom you have not gotten to know well. Open the door of your life "a crack" by sharing yourself with them. Don't force yourself upon the other. Just begin to open yourself within the natural relationships of life. Move only as far as you're invited to move. Allow the relationship to grow over a period of time.

3. When you feel ready, attempt to move some of your troubled relationships up to at least level 4. Remember that you are only responsible for your actions. You can only reach out with authentic love and invite people to join you in the upper levels of relationship.

4. Make it your personal goal to move all of your relationships to the upper levels. Practice the

lifestyle of at least opening the door of life a crack to everyone who comes into your life. Become known as a loving, honest, open, and affirming person who enjoys living the life of dialog!

EIGHT:
THE ENABLING SOURCE

KEY #7: *THE ENABLING SOURCE. We must allow God to be our enabling source in all of our communication!*

Throughout the earlier pages of this book, I have suggested that the major material on the "how to" of maximum communication would come in the last two chapters with the primary focus being presented in this, the final chapter. By now you have probably recognized the need for such a focus.

We have been discussing one of the most important subjects of our lives, and we have been suggesting some very difficult, even impossible, changes in our lifestyles. I have been moved deeply as I have been writing some of the exercises at the conclusion of each chapter. You can be assured that I understand just how difficult some of those exercises will be to fulfill in our lives.

We have obviously moved from the theoretical to the practical. We are not merely discussing pie in the sky. We are talking about the nitty-gritty of life and actual persons—you and me!

The bad news is that most of us do not communicate very well. In fact, if you have taken this book at all seriously, you will probably readily agree with me that we have a great deal of homework to do in becoming more effective communicators.

The good news is that all of us have the potential of becoming very effective communicators. How, then, do we master the art of experiencing and practicing maximum communication? We have begun by suggesting that we must understand the major components and principles of effective communication. That is what most of this book has been about. We need to understand the dynamics of transmitting and overcoming noise and listening and mirroring feelings and loving and dialoguing. We need to practice mastering the art of all those communication keys. That's why I have provided the exercises at the close of each chapter.

Knowing and practicing are vitally important. But probably most of us have concluded that those elements are simply not enough. We need something more. A human model would be of great help, but even such a model would not be adequate to meet our needs. We would be inspired by the model, but we need more than mere inspiration—we need enabling or empowering. Most of us are like a junior high runner who deeply desires to run a four-minute mile, but simply does not have the physical resources to pull it off. Or like the housewife who has the desire to purchase a $500 coat, but only has $45 available in her charge account.

The problem is not lack of knowledge or interest or desire. We simply do not have the personal resources to love or to communicate or to dialogue in the way in which we would like. We need help!

In searching the pages of literature and history, I have discovered the historical record of one unique group of people who enjoyed the life of authentic dialog. They were known by their love and their lifestyle of sharing. They actually enjoyed maximum communication.

THE LIFE OF DIALOG

The historical record of this remarkable group of people is found in Luke's account of the early Christian Church in the Acts of the Apostles, the fifth book of the New Testament. The second chapter of Acts shares an incredible and exciting story.

You will remember that after the crucifixion of Jesus, most of his followers were scattered. Many of them were literally hiding for their lives. Most of them were disillusioned and filled with despair. All of them were deeply grieved. Some three years earlier, they had forsaken all to follow Jesus. They believed that he was the Messiah, and that he was going to establish his Kingdom upon earth. They envisioned an immediate political kingdom which would overthrow the Roman rule. In fact, the favorite table topic of the twelve disciples concerned which of them would be the greatest in the new kingdom.

But now their dreams were shattered. Jesus was dead—and with him died their hopes for the new kingdom. But just as suddenly as their expectations had perished, the flames of hope were rekindled and burned more brightly than ever.

They were ecstatic to learn that Jesus was not dead; he had risen from the dead! He was alive! To be sure, some of them met the news with logical, scientific, and empirical skepticism. But he appeared to them and allowed them to touch him and to eat with him and to fellowship with him. (You may want to read the account for yourself in the closing chapters of John's Gospel.)

The Acts of the Apostles begins during the immediate post-resurrection period with a very interesting dialog between Jesus and his disciples.

Once again the disciples were interested in the coming of the kingdom. After all that had happened, they were sure the kingdom was about to be established. So they asked Jesus about it.

His answer confirmed that which he told them before his death. (See the Gospel of John, chapters 14–16) In short, he informed them that he could not tell them the precise details of the coming of the kingdom. But he assured them of a very wonderful fact: even though he must leave them to return to his Father, he would not leave them alone.

In fact, he stated, it would actually be expedient or good for them for him to leave, because God would come in another form to take his place. He spoke of the Holy Spirit who would not merely walk with them, but who would actually live in them and through them! He would be their helper and enabler!

The second chapter of the book of Acts relates the amazing fulfillment of that prophetic statement. This phenomenon began with a small group of Jesus' followers who had gathered together to pray in obedience to his instructions just before he ascended to be with his Father. As they were praying, the Holy Spirit came into their lives in a remarkable way.

The changes in the lives of these people were profound and immediate! For example, Peter, who had openly denied Jesus during his trial and who was in hiding during his crucifixion, now became bold and articulate. He and that little band of disciples went out into the streets of Jerusalem. Peter began to preach about the life, death, and resurrection of Jesus Christ and about the promise concerning the Holy Spirit.

Many of his listeners were so deeply cut to the heart that they asked Peter how they could be forgiven of their sins and receive the gift of the Holy Spirit. Peter invited them to repent and to be

99 The Enabling Source

baptized in the name of Jesus Christ for the forgiveness of their sins. And, he promised, they also would receive the Holy Spirit! Some 3,000 responded to that invitation! This, of course, was the birth of the Christian Church!

The reason I have taken time and space to review this unusual account is to focus on the unusual lifestyle of these early Christians. They immediately began to enjoy a spontaneous lifestyle of love and joy and peace and openness. The key descriptive word used to convey their relationships is the Greek word *koinonia,* which literally means *fellowship.* It is the spirit of generous sharing, of relating to one another in common or in community.

Actually, *koinonia* is the most perfect human example of what we have referred to as dialogical communication. It is the sharing of life with others in the deepest sense.

These people were described as "being together," "having all things in common," "sharing with those who had need," "sharing meals with spontaneous joy," "sharing authentic praise with God," and "being held in favor with all the people."

In short, they were enjoying the life of maximum communication—of dialogical lifestyle! To be sure, they knew nothing of communications theory or of sociological principles. But they experienced the real thing, that which we so often discuss in theory but are somehow never able to pull off.

I believe that the solution to this dilemma in our own lives is actually quite simple and is readily available to all of us. In addition to knowing the basics of communication and practicing the principles, we, too, need to be enabled to enjoy maximum communication!

As you have probably surmised, I believe that we need the enabling help of God himself. And like many others, I have found that such help is available to us now! We can enjoy the same lifestyle of authentic *koinonia* which was experienced by the early Christians.

THE SOLUTION

In order to discover the practicality of this enabling potential, we must begin by understanding the character of God and the character of humanity. The biblical record relates that in the beginning God created us in his own image. Man and woman enjoyed deep, fulfilling dialogical relationship with one another, with God, and with all creation. Everybody and everything enjoyed the life of perfect love and harmony!

Our problems began when we decided to leave that incredible relationship and to strike out on our own. We disobeyed God, turned our back on him, and determined to go our own way. With that action came alienation, selfishness, jealousy, separation, emptiness, discord, and ultimately death. We determined to do it our way—and we have paid a terrible price! That is what sin is all about (see Genesis 1–3).

But over the ages God has remained available to us as the aggressive lover. He has been willing to reestablish a relationship of love and trust and fellowship with us.

In fact, that is what the life of Jesus was all about. God so loved the world that he sent his only Son to provide the way for us to return to fellowship with him and with each other. The "Good News" (gospel) of the Bible is that God loves us so much that he came to live, to die, and to conquer death through his resurrection so that we could be restored to fellowship with him.

We cannot merit this relationship; we can neither earn it or learn it. It is a gift which we must receive by faith. The price which must be paid is for us to deny ourselves, turn from doing our own thing through faith in Christ, and then be committed to a life of following him (Mark 8:34).

As we repent and turn back to God, we are given the Holy Spirit to live in us and through us as our enabler and helper. We have the potential of loving and growing and communicating and living in wonderful fellowship with God and others.

Frankly, I know of no other way to enjoy the life of maximum communication. Until we are restored to open relationship with God and appropriate his enabling power, we will always fall short of what we really want or need to be. I believe that is precisely what Jesus meant when he said, "I am the way, the truth, and the life" (John 14:6).

Please understand that I am not propounding the doctrine of a given church or denomination. I am simply contending that all of us have the innate need to return to God and to enjoy fellowship with him. Only then can we become what we want to be and are trying to be. We simply cannot do it on our own. We need God's help and enabling power!

HOW TO LOVE

We need this same enabling in order to be able to love in the way in which we desire. As we were considering the characteristics of love in Chapter Six, we did not share the most basic definition of love, which is: "God is love." All that is good comes from God, and that includes love. If I am to love openly and unconditionally, if I am to risk pain and rejection, if I am to be a channel of authentic love, I need to be filled and enabled by God himself. Wherever there are fulfilling relationships, there is love; and wherever there is authentic love, there is God!

The reason that many of us have tried to become lovers and have failed is that we have tried to do it in our own way—without God. In fact, many of us have mistaken lust and sexual attraction for love.

When they have lost their luster and been expended, we mistakenly believe that love has waned. But love never wanes! When it is actively expressed, it grows and reproduces!

God offers us a potential for love which is beyond description. He is available to enable us to become genuine lovers. I am convinced that we can never become lovers without living in a vital, personal relationship with God, with ourselves, and with others. A lover has open communication upward, inward, and outward!

However, because God loves he does not force his way into our lives. He only loves and invites. His door is open to you. God is the only source of love, and only he can enable you to become a lover. It is your decision as to whether or not you want to open your life to him. He offers you the opportunity, but the choice is yours.

If you sense the need and the desire to turn to God and to be restored to fellowship and love with him, you have already taken the first step in that important decision—you have admitted your need and desire. This is what Jesus meant when he talked about denying ourselves. In so doing, we are admitting that we have been going the wrong way, and that we need God.

Secondly, we need to change direction. We need not only to admit we have been going the wrong way; we must turn from that way to God. By faith we must receive God's provision by allowing Christ to forgive us for going the way of sin, and we must entrust our lives to him!

Thirdly, we must then live out our new direction by following Jesus as the Lord or Master of our lives. Our primary concern will no longer be to do our own thing, but to do God's will. Our lives will be open to being filled with God in the person of the Holy Spirit.

And our lifestyles will become distinguished by

the fruit of the Spirit, which includes love, joy, peace, patience, kindness, goodness, faithfulness, gentleness, and self-control. Obviously, these are the qualities which we need in our lives if we are to practice and enjoy the life of love and dialog! These qualities cannot be fabricated or bought at any price; they can only come from God!

LIVING THE LIFE

Lest we close this book in Camelot or with us riding off into the sunset to live happily ever after, let us build all that we have shared upon the foundations of reality. I have been speaking consistently about the potential of love and of dialogical communication. The potential of such a lifestyle is available to all of us. However, as I have said from the beginning, the path is not an easy one.

What a delight it is to know that we do not have to do it alone. We have Almighty God to enable us! And we have one another! In fact, that is what the authentic Church is all about. It is more than an organization or institution or a specific denomination.

The true Church is comprised of a band of people who have turned from their way to Christ, and who are attempting to follow him as Lord day by day. Such persons are open to God, to each other, to others, and to all of creation. They have not arrived; they are *becoming*! Every day they are growing to become more the person which God created them to be, but which sin has prevented them from being.

They are committed to God's lifestyle, which is characterized by love and open communication and all that is good! The doors of their lives are open for dialogical communication—*koinonia*.

They are involved in growing through communicating more clearly, overcoming noise, listening, mirroring feelings, loving, and dialoguing. And they are constantly available to encourage and assist one another.

Wouldn't you like to be a part of that kind of Church? Well, you can be. Allow God to begin with you. Be sensitive and open to others who are of a like mind and heart. Don't fall into the trap of becoming judgmental and aloof. If you are now involved in a church, don't become a problem; be used of God to be a solution in the lives of others. As you attempt to live the authentic life of love and openness, God will guide you and use you. What he is doing for you, he will do for others. You can help and encourage each other and invite others to share with you!

THE ENABLING SOURCE

In summary, we must allow God to be our enabling source in all of our communication! That is the seventh and primary key for maximum communication.

Such enabling is available to us day by day. For example, as you engage in the exercises at the end of si . chapters of this book, don't attempt to complete them in your own strength. Ask God to help you. He will enable you to do exceeding more than you ever thought possible. The joy and excitement of such an experience defies description!

At the beginning of this book I promised to share seven principles of communication which could literally change your life! I also stated that there are no quick or easy shortcuts to the life of communion.

The key words in each of the seven principles spell *COMMUNE*! Be sure to memorize that outline and the seven keys! Memorizing the keys is important. But of much more importance is this: What are you going to do with them?

Life has the potential of being a wonderful banquet. The table has been prepared for all who would come and commune. You have been invited to the delightful life of maximum communication. Why not join me in responding to the loving invitation to *COMMUNE*!